More SECRETS of My SPECTRUM

By
Callum Knight

Copyright © 2025 Frami Books
www.framibooks.com

All rights reserved. This publication may not be reproduced, stored in a retrieval system, or transmitted in any form or by any means—electronic, mechanical, photocopying, recording, or otherwise—without the prior written permission of the publisher.

No part of this book may be used or reproduced in any manner for the purpose of training artificial intelligence technologies or systems without the express written permission of the publisher. The publisher expressly reserves all rights with respect to text and data mining. DSM Directive 2019/790, referencing Article 5(3), makes no exception.

ISBN: 978-1-917514-18-7

Cover design & typeset by Callum Knight

Published by Frami Books

A catalogue record for this book is available from the British Library.

First published in 2025

DEDICATION

To the readers who first discovered *The Secrets of My Spectrum* and found pieces of their own story within mine, thank you for giving me the courage to keep writing.

To families, friends, teachers, and supporters who pick up this book in the hope of understanding autism more deeply, your willingness to learn is the greatest gift you can give.

And to every autistic person who has ever felt unseen: this book is for you. May it remind you that your experiences matter, your voice is important, and your spectrum holds its own unique secrets worth celebrating.

CONTENTS

Introduction	1
Finding My Place in the World	3
Understanding	11
Responsibilities	17
Masking & Why It's Exhausting	25
Social Life & Relationships	35
Celebrating	59
When It Finally Clicks	65
Mental Health & Self-Care	69
Facing Life Changes	87
Learning To Drive	93
Handling the Unexpected	113
Learning Self-Advocacy	121
Finding Calm in My Interests	125
Why I Can One Day & Not the Next	133
Education	139
Final Thoughts	151
About The Author	155
Crisis & Helpful People	157

INTRODUCTION

This book continues the story I began in *The Secrets of My Spectrum*, which I wrote when I was sixteen to share my autistic experiences up to that age.

Now, I'm sharing more insights into my life up to twenty-one: the difficulties I've overcome, the challenges I'm still facing, and the new situations that have shaped my life since, including transitioning into adulthood, navigating education, and ultimately becoming self-employed.

I wrote *The Secrets of My Spectrum* because I wasn't sure how to explain my autism to my family and friends, and I hoped it might also help other young people like me, giving them something to share with their own families to deepen their understanding of what it's like to grow up with autism.

By sharing both the strategies that helped me and the struggles I faced day to day, I wanted to start a conversation about the complexities of living life as an autistic child.

I'm deeply grateful for the support that book received, and for the encouragement and confidence it gave me to write this one. My hope is that this book offers just as much helpful insight. If you're discovering my writing for the first time, I hope this book gives you a window into autism that feels personal and real.

FINDING MY PLACE IN THE WORLD

I used to worry a lot about growing up and becoming an adult. The responsibilities and expectations felt overwhelming, and I wasn't sure if I'd be able to manage them all. But now that I'm older, I've realised that adulthood isn't something that happens overnight. It's a gradual process, and not everything gets easier all at once.

I always say that every autistic person is different. Although we share many of the same challenges, we don't all experience them in the same way or to the same degree. One person's struggle might not be a problem for someone else, and whether a challenge prevents us from completing a task entirely or becomes something we can overcome in time depends on our personal abilities, current situations, and level of support. Some things I thought would be impossible for me at sixteen have not only turned out to be possible, but now they feel normal.

I may not have gone about things in the most conventional way, but I've chosen my own path. With help and support, I've succeeded in areas I never thought I could, even just a couple of years ago. An autism diagnosis doesn't tell you everything about someone who is autistic. It highlights traits such as sensory sensitivities, anxiety, or literal thinking and communication challenges, but each autistic person has their own way of experiencing and managing these.

Someone else might not share my anxieties or have the same learning challenges I do. If you genuinely want to support the autistic person in your life, you need to take the time to understand them as an individual. Autism is a spectrum, not a script. No two stories are the same. When you see the person, not just the diagnosis, that's when the real support begins.

If you're not autistic yourself, you can't be expected to take a course and magically understand every autistic person. It isn't like maths, where it adds up or it doesn't. I talk about my challenges, and it's wonderful when people relate and feel better about themselves, but I also need to acknowledge those who don't see the world the way that I do.

They may struggle in different ways and might not relate to my specific challenges at all. That's why I want to make it clear: I'm not trying to speak for every autistic person. I can only talk about how autism affects me. That's why I have included notes pages at the end of the chapters in *The Secrets of My Spectrum* and in this book too, so that you or your loved ones can write down the challenges that affect you and find ways to help. We all have different secrets to our spectrum, and we all need the time, space, and care to feel safe enough to unmask them. I hope these pages can help you learn more about yourself as an individual, your needs, and how being autistic affects you.

Autism difficulties can compound. I might cope with one or two challenges in a day, but adding more, whether from family expectations, being around someone I'm not comfortable with, or dealing with unkindness or misunderstanding, can propel me into a meltdown. When I meltdown, it isn't always obvious because it happens internally.

If I can't pull myself out of it, I fall into a shutdown. You may be reading this, thinking you've tried a million ways to prevent yourself from going into a meltdown, and it isn't possible to pull yourself out, and you may be right. From talking to other autistic people, I've learned that some of us find it much more challenging, even almost impossible, to prevent it. But as I've grown up, I've found ways to pull myself out of a shutdown, and I'll talk more about this throughout the book.

As cars are my favourite subject, I'm going to use them to explain what I mean in more detail. Sometimes, for no reason at all, I'll wake up in the morning and feel like I'm in the wrong gear. Nothing I do works, and no matter how hard I try, I'm stuck in that gear and can't achieve the goal I want. It's frustrating and upsetting. On days like that, I need help with almost every task.

It isn't that I don't want to do things, I do. It isn't laziness or a choice to stay in bed instead of doing something important. It feels more like a vital component inside my brain has been removed. I feel stuck, even though I want to move forward. On other days, it feels like my brain glides into first gear with no trouble at all, and tasks seem easier somehow. Why? I don't have a clue!

What I've learned is that every day, whether I'm stuck in first or cruising in fifth, all that matters is that I keep trying.

~ A page for your thoughts ~

UNDERSTANDING

I've often been asked whether I'm glad I was told I'm autistic after my diagnosis. The answer is yes, because knowing helped me understand why I struggled in certain areas of my life and why I couldn't always meet expectations. I always knew it wasn't about me not trying hard enough, because I always did my best. So to find out that my brain is literally wired differently was a huge relief.

Without that understanding, I believe I would have fallen into self-doubt and possibly developed mental health struggles, because I would have thought the problem was me. In education, standard curriculum workbooks often confused me. The information was there, but my interpretation of it wasn't always correct. My mum found creative ways to help facilitate my learning, such as using cars and games to help me better understand concepts. I also needed a lot of repetition. Sometimes, I needed her to repeat a question or explain it differently several times before I truly understood what the lesson was trying to teach me.

It was a relief to my mum to receive my diagnosis too, because up until then, she was really worried that she was failing me. The relief came in understanding that the problem wasn't whether I was capable, but whether I was given an approach that worked for me. Knowing it wasn't my fault that I struggled to understand definitely helped.

The adults in my life who expected me to thrive using neurotypical methods found out quite quickly that they might as well have been putting diesel in a petrol engine. There's nothing wrong with the fuel or the engine; they're just incompatible. When I understood that, I could concentrate on what my brain did well instead of what it didn't. This applies not only to education but also to learning how to navigate the world around me and understanding my sensory struggles and social challenges, rather than criticising myself for them.

I've been told that for many, receiving a diagnosis is inaccessible or a long, complicated process, so I understand why some people self-identify as autistic.

Sometimes people have also been misdiagnosed. Professionals don't always get it right. My younger brother displayed far more obvious signs of autism when we were younger. Yet, he was misdiagnosed at ten years old with Generalised Anxiety Disorder. One of the reasons my mum was given for this was that younger siblings often copy behaviours, and because I was autistic, she thought that explained his behaviour. Although that didn't explain the learning difficulties he had, which were always much more challenging for him than mine were for me.

When he was in his late teens, my mum sought a second opinion, and that was when a specialist diagnosed him with autism spectrum disorder with a PDA profile (Pathological Demand Avoidance). So, if you have been given a misdiagnosis, you're not alone.

Getting my diagnosis didn't change who I am. It helped me understand myself in a way I never could before. It gave me the language to explain things I'd always felt but couldn't put into words. And most importantly, it reminded me that I wasn't broken; I just needed the right kind of support. That understanding has made all the difference.

~ A page for your thoughts ~

RESPONSIBILITIES

As a teenager, I often worried about how life would be for me growing up. I wasn't sure if I'd be able to handle all the things that would be expected of me, such as becoming independent, taking on larger responsibilities, and learning to navigate the world confidently. It all felt incredibly overwhelming at the time.

But some things have become a little bit easier for me now, like brief social interactions and day-to-day tasks, such as taking our dog for a walk or going to the supermarket. I've made a routine of remembering to set timers when I'm running a bath or making something to eat. I've had a couple of mishaps, most recently with the hose, forgetting to switch it off and coming home to a flooded garden because I was filling up a paddling pool for my dog in the soaring heat. If I could speak to my sixteen-year-old self now, I would say, 'Don't worry so much about the things you'll have to go through when you're older, because many things that feel impossible now will come more naturally as you gain more life experience.'

The things you aren't able to do now, you'll find ways to manage, whether by finding the right support or by taking on the challenge of learning day by day, step-by-step. It isn't all as overwhelming as you now fear. You'll become a more confident person and learn to be more independent.

You need to take it one day at a time and remember to celebrate the small wins, because they are the foundations for the bigger ones. Of course, there are some things that haven't changed at all. I'm still autistic, so I have the same challenges that come with that, and there are some things I still dread, like phone calls. I'm expected to make them and take them more now, and almost every time I feel as though I can't talk. I freeze up, and my brain blanks.

Phone calls are something I'm still not comfortable with, but every time I make one, it gets slightly easier and less stressful. I'm working on it, even though it's a slow process. On a positive note, I'm fine calling my family now, although I still struggle on the bad days. I'm still working on those unexpected phone calls from strangers or when I'm calling businesses, which is terrifying.

It makes me sad that I struggle so much with communication. I've been invited to podcasts and radio shows, to speak at schools, and to meet readers who relate to my experiences through my books. I'd love to connect with people, but the thought of putting myself in those situations makes me really anxious. The hardest part is feeling like I'm letting people down. I rarely feel safe speaking freely because I need time to process what I want to say and how I want to say it. Once something's said out loud, I can't take it back, so I'm always conscious of how my words might come across.

My younger brother, who you know is also autistic (though very different from me), struggles with this too. Sometimes he comes across as insulting or disrespectful, even though that's not what he means. We often help him rephrase words because the words he uses don't always match what he's trying to express. While he's less aware of it, I have a deep fear of being misunderstood.

I really appreciate receiving emails from readers. They're always so kind, and their messages leave me feeling both grateful and humbled. Many people have shared personal challenges with me, and when I hear that my experiences have helped them see things from a new perspective, it means a lot. It's also easy to tell when someone has read my book, because they often mention that they don't expect a reply. I always want to respond, because it's incredibly thoughtful of them to reach out. But I also appreciate that they take the pressure off me, allowing me to reply in my own time without feeling guilty. I have to remind myself that all these experiences will ultimately help me deal with those situations better in the future.

I couldn't do this as a child. I didn't have the ability to put a positive spin on it, but I've recently learned to use these experiences to help me in new situations. And I try to use confident days as an opportunity to improve my social skills.

I've learned it's not healthy to overthink every interaction I've had and dwell on them, but

I can't always control how my mind works. I know intellectually how silly that is, but I can't turn it off.

So sometimes, I just don't feel able to go to the shops and pick up a loaf of bread or get a stamp at the post office. These are simple things I'd normally be expected to do as an adult, and yet they're still a very real struggle for me.

~ A page for your thoughts ~

MASKING & WHY IT'S EXHAUSTING

As a child, I learned quickly that stimming made me stand out, so I would mask. Unless you know me really well, you wouldn't notice me struggling, because I can mask my emotions so well. This means I often come across as neurotypical to people around me, and unless something unexpected happens and my mask falls, you wouldn't know that I'm autistic.

For example, I'm able to respond politely to people and engage in friendly small talk at the tills when I'm paying for something, and I can maintain eye contact for short periods of time. It was an eye-opener for me when I was

little and heard that people who don't make
eye contact are often seen as untrustworthy.
I'd hate to be thought of that way, because I'm
a very honest person. Recently, I told someone
that I'm autistic, and they said that they
wouldn't have guessed because I made such
good eye contact.

The thing is, I can't do it for long. I will have
to look away usually at some points during
the conversation, but I think it's important
to mention it, because from what I've heard
a lot of autistic people have mastered the
art of eye contact or at least, seeming to
others that they are. It isn't that we can't
be taught to do it; it's that doing it is very
uncomfortable. My brother described how
it felt to him, like someone looking into his
soul, which is exactly how it feels to me; it's
almost invasive.

Depending on the level of concentration I
need at the time, looking at someone can be

counterproductive. So, the old-fashioned 'look at me when I'm talking to you' was never effective on me as a child because the minute I was expected to look at someone, I couldn't process any of what they said after that; I was too busy concentrating on trying to look in their eyes.

As I've grown up, eye contact has become easier. Another is facial expressions. I try to make sure I smile and don't blankly stare at people. I also tend to mimic the body language of the person I'm talking to, almost like I'm copying their characteristics. I'm somehow able to do all that, but one thing I struggle with is holding conversations.

If someone speaks to me, I'll answer them, but I do struggle to keep a conversation going most of the time. When I reach the awkward silence stage of a conversation, I try to think of a way to continue it. However, I usually get caught up trying to decide what socially acceptable question to ask next, and by the time I do, the conversation has moved on to something else. I don't mask because I'm embarrassed about being autistic. It's more about the kind of day I'm having, what's happening around me and whether the person I'm interacting with truly understands autism and how it can affect me.

The last thing I want is for someone to make assumptions about what I can or can't do based on limited information about me.

Masking helps me navigate social situations more easily and without drawing attention to myself, as everyone now knows that I am really uncomfortable in most social situations and hate standing out.

But, on the other hand, masking also gives me the feeling of impostor syndrome. Because I mask so well, there are even times, despite everything I've told you about how autism affects me and how many challenges it brings, I can even fool myself into thinking I'm more capable than I actually am!

Some days, I find tasks easier because I'm having a good day and everything is going smoothly. As I explained earlier, it's as though my brain has moved into first gear without any problems at all, and I'm ready to get on with my day with a clear road ahead on a bright, sunny morning.

In my head, I've come across as though I'm not autistic at all, and then the guilt sets in. I start questioning whether I truly need the help I've been given, wondering if I'm imagining my struggles or just not handling them as well as everyone else.

And then, on other days, I realise why I need the help I get because I can't even walk into a shop without the slightest unexpected encounter throwing me into a shutdown;

sometimes, if I'm going to the shops and I plan to buy a specific item but an area is closed off, the self-checkouts aren't working, or the item is sold out, I can fall into a kind of zombie-like state, my brain is stuck in processing, and I'm merely a passenger waiting for my internal information board to show my next destination.

I am literally wandering around the shop aimlessly, not knowing how to deal with it, yet on other days, random, unexpected encounters can be fine. I wish I could tell you why this happens. I wish I could explain it and understand myself, but I don't. As I said, it's as though there is a missing component in my brain that causes me to get stuck, and I struggle to find a route out.

I often find myself putting on a persona and dressing in a way I think will make people take me seriously. But on days when I'm struggling, that effort can backfire; I might come across as rude, strange, or even odd because no one can see that I'm autistic. So, masking can make life more challenging for me. The support I might need becomes invisible because, to others, it appears that I'm managing just fine.

This disconnect means that what's actually going on in my head isn't visible to those around me. When I leave the house from day to day, I will prepare for what I'm going to be doing, like random chit-chat when I'm at tills, smiling if I make eye contact with anyone, and remembering my list so I don't end up walking into a shop and completely forgetting why I'm there!

So, while I might seem like I'm coping from the outside, there's often a lot going on beneath the surface, struggles that aren't visible, but very real to me. Masking helps me get through the day, but it also hides the parts of me that need the most understanding.

MORE SECRETS OF MY SPECTRUM

I don't mask because I want to pretend I'm someone else; I do it because it helps me feel safe and blend in.

~ A page for your thoughts ~

SOCIAL LIFE & RELATIONSHIPS

Because I'm tall, people in the supermarket sometimes ask me to reach items from the top shelf for them. I don't mind that; it's a quick interaction, and I like being able to help. But outside those simple moments, offering help can feel much harder. When the situation isn't straightforward, my anxiety kicks in, and suddenly what should be a kind gesture feels like a risk.

I often wish I could offer to help people more proactively, but I'm not always sure what's socially acceptable. I worry that approaching someone might come across as rude or sarcastic, even though my intentions are kind.

For example, I recently saw a neighbour pulling weeds from their driveway by hand. I'd just bought a tool that would make the job easier, and I wanted to lend it to them, but I didn't feel confident enough to offer it to them. Instead, I mentioned it to my brother, who lent it to them on my behalf.

My brother's autism doesn't affect his social communication as much as mine does. He can chat with people more easily, both in person and online, and it amazes me how naturally he joins groups and builds friendships. Although I do have online friends, I'm unable to join voice chats and talk to people I don't know in the way that he can. For me, those situations feel overwhelming, like stepping into a spotlight I'm not ready for.

This contrast shows how autism isn't one single experience; our strengths and challenges can look very different, even within the same family. Sometimes he has a look about him that gives the impression he's unapproachable, even when he's in a really good mood. I often notice people avoiding him. By comparison, even when I don't feel very sociable, I can usually keep a smile on my face and make small talk if someone speaks to me for a short time. In that way, he can be wonderfully friendly or quite intimidating, whereas I usually come across as more laid back, regardless of how I'm feeling.

Everyone feels anxious at times. But as Dr Michelle Garnett explains, autistic anxiety is different because the amygdala works in another way. She says: *'When you are autistic, your amygdala is working differently. It is structurally different and functionally different, and this means we have a bigger fear reaction.*

We are beginning to understand autistic anxiety as fear-based, which makes it far more taxing on the body. There are huge physiological reactions, more avoidance, and more sensory overload. If you are in a fear response a lot, your body is impacted. The autonomic nervous system becomes dysregulated. That means our normal balance in the body is not working, and we stay anxious and fearful for longer. The problem keeps going, making autistic people more susceptible to mental health conditions, physical health conditions, and trauma.'

For me, anxiety doesn't just feel like butterflies in the stomach; it's more like a full-body alarm. It's the kind of fear that makes me avoid things because it feels like walking along a cliff edge with no barrier. The ground is uneven, the wind is strong, and one wrong step could mean falling. In that moment, your body screams: 'This is unsafe, you could die if you make a mistake.'

I know this sounds dramatic, but on bad days, that's the reality of how my body responds to anxiety. Small interactions can feel like danger. Asking for help or offering it isn't just uncomfortable; it can feel impossible. The fear is so strong that even when kindness is my intention, silence feels safer. I've been trying my best to navigate this throughout my life, but the hardest part is that the feeling can appear out of nowhere.

Like when I was walking out of a shop, and someone near me shouted, 'Excuse me!' Suddenly, I'm hit with that fight or flight response, and it's really frustrating. On the brighter side, when I'm having a good day, it's much more manageable, but I never truly know how I'll feel until I'm in the situation.

That unpredictability is what makes autistic anxiety so exhausting. It's not just about feeling nervous; I'm living with a brain that can react as if normal interactions are dangerous.

'Sticky brain syndrome' is a term my family uses to describe those moments when a thought or experience from the day gets stuck in my mind. I can't shake it, and it starts to push me towards a meltdown. It's our way of naming that feeling when something just won't let go, no matter how much I try to ignore it or stop overthinking it.

Sometimes I feel like everything has gone wrong, or at least not how I expected it to go, and it sends me into this strange in–between state. It's not quite a meltdown, but it's intense enough that I can't stop replaying certain moments from the day. They get stuck in my mind, tormenting me, and I struggle to let them go.

When that happens, I've found that having a shower or a bath really helps me. It gives me space to breathe and to think things through. It's like I'm washing the day off, physically and mentally, and most of the time it works.

I come out feeling clearer and more grounded. Now that I'm older, I'm better at putting these feelings into words. Even so, it's still hard to explain. There's a depth to it that doesn't always translate out loud.

Friendships & Social Groups

One thing that surprised my family was when I told them I'm quite happy by myself, and I don't feel lonely when I'm on my own.

When I was told that most people don't like being alone, and that they prefer to be with lots of friends, socialising and taking part in group activities, I remember wondering: Why? Because I've always been content in my own company.

I know we're all different, and some people won't feel the same as I do. However, for me, being alone is peaceful. I enjoy having time to myself and the freedom to do whatever I want without having to entertain others or carry the pressure of making sure they're enjoying themselves too. Because of the way I am, I often wonder why so many people are concerned about how many friends an autistic person has. I care about my friends, but that doesn't mean I want them to be involved in every part of my life.

As I've grown up, I've realised that just because other people seem to be having fun going out with friends or going to the cinema, it doesn't mean I'd have the same experience if I joined them. Sometimes, the pressure to enjoy the same experiences as neurotypical people can be more about expectation than actual enjoyment. I've had to explain to family and friends that I'm quite happy not doing some of those things.

I rarely enjoy spontaneous social meet-ups or interacting with people I don't know very well. I often find those situations draining, leaving me feeling detached and disconnected, as if I'm observing from the outside rather than truly taking part. With new people, I'm always trying to gauge what they're like as a person and whether we connect, which makes it hard to relax into a conversation.

For me, socialising isn't just about being around people for the sake of being present in a group. It's about finding genuine shared interests, building trust, and forming an honest connection. When I enjoy spending time alone or need deeper, more meaningful friendships to feel comfortable, I'm not going to enjoy large, casual social gatherings. Just being in a crowd doesn't automatically make me feel less lonely.

I might not always enjoy loud places, major events, or certain types of travel, but enjoying time alone doesn't mean I'm not sociable; it just means I socialise differently.

MORE SECRETS OF MY SPECTRUM

Personal Relationship Dynamics

There seems to be a lot of social pressure around being in a romantic relationship, especially among teenagers and young adults. Whenever I hadn't seen extended family for a while, one of the first things they'd ask me was whether I had a girlfriend yet. Because of that, I can understand why some people might question themselves if they're not interested in dating yet, especially when everyone around them seems to be making a relationship a priority.

A lot of people my age are actively looking for relationships or feel like they should be, but I don't feel that way. It's not that I'm not ready for a relationship; I just know I only want one if it feels right. I'm happy to wait for someone who truly aligns with who I am, however long that takes. I would need time to meet and truly get to know someone before intimacy even becomes a question. I want to meet someone with the same values as me. I have no idea how anyone is expected to know if they're attracted to someone based on a photograph, either, like with dating apps.

For me, I need to build a friendship first before even considering that. And at twenty-one, I have no interest in making a relationship a priority. If I meet someone, that's great, but I'm not actively looking. I think most people will know when they're ready, and I don't think anyone should feel pressured or be made to feel odd just because they've reached a certain age and don't want to date anyone yet, especially if they're still figuring out who they are and what they want from a relationship. If anything, that seems like the more mature option to me.

I know that if I had been in school or constantly around my own age group and they were focused on relationships, social pressure might have made me feel like there was something wrong with me. So, to anyone who feels the same way I do: if relationships aren't a priority for you right now, or you're simply not interested in anyone, you're not alone.

After speaking to other autistic adults, I found that many of them didn't develop an interest in relationships until later in life, after years of feeling as though they'll never meet anyone they'd feel a connection with.

I think the most important relationship we should prioritise is the one with ourselves. For me, that's the foundation for a healthy relationship. I believe it's essential to have respect for yourself because when we respect, trust, and value ourselves, it not only sets healthy boundaries for the kind of people we let into our lives, but it can also significantly improve our own lives too.

I recently heard a phrase that made me laugh: 'You can't be everyone's cup of tea, or you'd be a mug!' It stuck with me because it's so true. We're not always going to get along with everyone, but I believe acceptance and kindness make a difference. And if I don't receive that from somebody, I try not to take it personally.

When people on the spectrum have written to me about the difficult things they've gone through, it's heartbreaking. What really gets to me is that so many of them seem to carry guilt or shame about things that weren't their fault. I know misunderstandings happen a lot when you communicate or process things differently, but that still doesn't give anyone permission to be cruel. Some people just aren't kind, and I don't think there's anything wrong with keeping your distance from those people.

Sometimes that's just what you need to feel safe. Oddly, despite writing books about my life experiences, I'm quite a private person. I don't post much about my life on social media sites, and I only really use Facebook for my author page. That doesn't mean I don't share any aspects of my life with people; it just means I prefer not to share every aspect of it online for just anyone to see.

Instead, I choose to focus on what truly matters to me: my personal growth, embracing who I am, and valuing myself on my own terms–not what social media says I should have, need, or want.

One thing I try to remember is that what one person sees as success might not align with what success means to you. Success is the achievement of **your** goals, not anyone else's. I try to remind myself of this and stay focused on my own path. It's very easy to see posts on social media and assume that unless you are doing the same, you have somehow failed or are falling behind. I think it's important to remember not to get caught up in that mindset because it's extremely destructive.

SOCIAL LIFE & RELATIONSHIPS

Different Ways to Connect

If someone had asked me what socialising meant to me when I was younger, I think it could have opened up a more helpful conversation. Even if I felt lonely at times, being put into a club or with a group of people I didn't know didn't necessarily help.

In fact, it often made me feel even lonelier, because I was surrounded by people who didn't understand me. My mum tried to help by putting me in more social situations, thinking it would help me connect with people. But in reality, it just made me feel more unhappy and less sociable.

I was often quite content entertaining myself at home. Being forced into social spaces that didn't suit me only made me feel more like an outcast, and it reinforced the idea that there was something wrong with me.

In my first book, I talked about being signed up for gymnastics and drama clubs as a child. While I enjoyed those activities, I'd often be watching other kids connect with each other so easily, while I felt completely invisible. It was hard.

It wasn't that I didn't want to socialise. I often did. But I didn't want to socialise the way they did. I didn't enjoy talking about the same things or doing the same activities as them, and it became more obvious to me that I was different.

Connections That Count

When I was younger, I found that I only really enjoyed spending time with other kids my age if we shared a genuine interest. If I wasn't interested in the activity, simply being around people didn't make me feel more sociable or help me connect. When I'm with people who share an interest, I feel more at ease and can join in. But if the focus shifts to something completely different, like a party or a noisy social event, I'd feel uncomfortable and out of place. Unless other people understand my difficulties and are willing to include me, it is very difficult to feel part of the group.

Structured lessons or activities were easier for me to cope with. But the moment it was break time, everything changed. Suddenly, I was expected to use social skills I didn't naturally have. That was often a lonely and overwhelming experience, and it usually went unnoticed by others. Ironically, it was the time when I most needed support, yet it was also the time when I was left only with other children, feeling stressed, anxious, and completely alone.

My brother had similar struggles. Unlike me, he bravely tried to join challenging after-school clubs and groups. My mum would ask leaders and teachers to give him a small job during break times, like loading a car or putting things away, something to give him purpose in those unstructured moments. But he still found making connections hard. He was often approached by girls who wanted his attention, and he was left floundering, unable to understand their attempts at conversation. The giggling and odd questions made him extremely uncomfortable.

I felt sad for him. It took a lot of courage to put himself in those situations, something I would never have been brave enough to try. Yet it turned out to be more damaging to his confidence than not trying at all, because he blamed himself when things fell apart instead of realising that those kinds of social interactions weren't suitable for him.

Unfortunately, the adults didn't always understand what he needed or follow through with what my mum had asked, so he wasn't supported in the way he needed. For me, socialisation often didn't feel enjoyable. At times, it felt more like a punishment. That's how overwhelming it could be, and sometimes it even became mentally damaging.

I've learned that expecting me to pick up social skills just by being around others was unrealistic. It was like handing me a musical instrument and assuming I'd learn to play it simply by sitting with the band.

Without proper instruction and guidance, I wouldn't suddenly know how to read music, coordinate with others, or produce a melody. Social skills worked in a similar way for me. I didn't develop them automatically through exposure; I needed support and guided learning.

I was lucky in our home education groups. Our parents were always there, which gave me a chance to check in, ask questions, and observe social interactions in a way that felt safe. We got to know and trust each other's parents, and they played a significant role in helping me feel comfortable just being myself. That supportive space helped me learn how to socialise in a way that worked for me. I was much more comfortable around them than I ever was around kids my own age.

Growing up, I noticed that kids who went to school often had a very different dynamic. There seemed to be more of a hierarchy. In our social group, that wasn't the case. Younger kids were respected as much as older ones, and we all took part in activities together. We genuinely cared about each other. If someone was being reckless or looked like they were struggling, we'd let one of the parents know, not to get them into trouble, but because we wanted them to be okay.

If someone was in the group, they were one of us, and we looked out for each other. I've never experienced this in groups run

SOCIAL LIFE & RELATIONSHIPS

by government organisations, which I find interesting. What struck me most was how different those groups felt compared to ours. When I was with school friends, it seems they thought it was normal to push someone out or assert control over the youngest or quietest person in the group. That always confused me, because those who appeared more vulnerable were the ones we felt most protective of in our groups.

I was grateful not to have grown up with that kind of social experience. I don't think I would have coped very well with it. That version of socialisation, where people are left out or made to feel small, didn't feel social to me at all. To my brother and me, it felt anti-social.

We always knew we weren't the most sociable kids in the traditional sense, but at least we hadn't learned how to be unkind. Once I trust someone and feel comfortable in their company, I can actually become quite extroverted. Lately, I'm more comfortable reaching out to people I have known a long time via text; But forming those friendships in the first place is the hard part. It takes time to build trust, and when making connections is already difficult, it can feel isolating when there don't seem to be many opportunities to meet new people.

I've also realised that you don't have to be autistic to struggle with forming deep connections. In 2018, the Movember Foundation reported that approximately 27% of men in the UK had no close friends. A You. Gov study found that 26% of women in the UK also didn't have a 'best friend'. That showed me that this difficulty isn't exclusive to autism.

For me, social interactions are often more challenging because of my differences in communication and how I understand social norms. But I remind myself that not having close friendships doesn't make me unworthy or a failure. It's something many people experience, and that's okay.

~ A page for your thoughts ~

CELEBRATING

I turned eighteen right in the middle of lockdown, and honestly, it worked out well for me. It took away all the pressure of having to do something special or meet expectations.

Every year, I'm asked if I'd like to travel or have extended family over, but I'm perfectly happy treating it as any other day.
When I turned twenty and lockdown was over, I felt that pressure again, so I invited a few family members over. But honestly, I would have been just as happy washing my car!

If I told someone I spent my birthday doing that, they might think I hadn't enjoyed myself or even feel sorry for me – but that would have been an excellent birthday for me. Doing something I actually enjoy makes more sense than going along with a big gathering, spending time with relatives I don't know well, or heading to a pub for a drink. It doesn't mean I never enjoy those things, but sometimes it's too much fuss and I wonder if it's really worth it.

I do sometimes worry that I'm missing out, but the truth is I wouldn't have enjoyed it anyway. So I'm totally fine celebrating in my own way.

As I've grown up, I've realised the gifts I ask for are a bit unusual too. I appreciate things related to my interests. When I got into car detailing, I asked for car detailing products and buckets for Christmas. You should have seen my grandmother's face when I unwrapped a set of car detailing brushes from my mum!

But I was over the moon. They're expensive, and they're something I'll actually use and appreciate. I've also found that opening gifts in front of people has become easier, probably because I usually have a good idea of what I'm getting. In our house, we send each other links to gifts we'd really like, and our family picks something from the list. It works well for us. I always feel terrible if someone buys me something that ends up sitting in a cupboard unused. I'd rather they spend that money on something useful or something they need themselves.

My brother has a very different approach to gifts. He dislikes what he calls 'utility' presents and only wants things he's specifically asked for. Up until recently, he wouldn't let anyone buy him anything he hadn't already pre-approved.

If he opened something he wasn't expecting, he'd get frustrated and have a meltdown. It wasn't because he wasn't grateful, but because he felt guilty that someone had spent money on something he didn't want. To him, it felt like a waste, and it made him feel bad that someone had essentially wasted their money on him. Now that he's older, he's more open to small surprises, as long as they relate to his special interests. But that's where he draws the line.

My mum will often show me things she's thinking of buying, and if I like them, she'll get them, wrap them, and put them under the tree at Christmas. I find that much easier because I know what to expect, and I've usually forgotten about it by the time Christmas arrives.

As a child, Christmas, gifts, plans, and food often caused major confusion around family. For a few years, my mum adapted to this by celebrating on the 24th instead. Since she's half Swedish and her family traditionally celebrates then, she thought it might work better for us. It actually did, for a while. There was no pressure to go to sleep early or wake up at a specific time, and we could choose what we wanted to eat. Some years, we didn't even have a Christmas dinner; we just ate whatever meal we wanted. My brother and I always struggled to sleep on Christmas Eve, so this setup worked well when we were younger.

However, as we grew up, my brother especially came to embrace the traditions of a British Christmas. Now he wants everything to be the same as everyone else. I think the important thing for us is to accept that celebrations don't have to look the same for everyone; what matters is that it feels right for you.

~ A page for your thoughts ~

WHEN IT FINALLY CLICKS

As I've gotten older, I've realised that context is really important for me. My brother is the same; he needs specific context when he's asked to do something or follow instructions.

I remember once seeing someone online trying to teach a child how to fold clothes. On the surface, it seemed like a good idea, but as I was watching, it just didn't sit right with me. They took the child into their bedroom, opened a drawer of perfectly folded clothes, pulled them out, and chucked them onto the bed. Then they started folding them again, showing the child how, before putting them back in the drawer. As a child, I would have been completely confused by that. Why take clothes that are already folded, only to unfold them again? To me, the lesson wouldn't have been obvious. All I would have understood was that someone had taken out clothes, messed them up, and now they were asking me to fix their problem. I wasn't surprised when the child became angry and frustrated.

If I'd been taught life skills like that, I would have needed it to be done in a way that made sense and felt relevant to everyday life. When I understand the purpose behind something, it's much easier for me to engage with it.

For example, instead of taking clothes out of the drawer, I would have understood better if they'd been taken off the washing line or out of the tumble dryer. That way, I would have been helping with something real instead of doing what felt like a pointless exercise.
It reminds me of when I was learning English as a child. When I was asked to read a paragraph and then put it into my own words, I

could never understand why. I get it now. The idea was to prove I understood the text, but back then, it just seemed like a complete waste of my time. Why would I spend ages rewriting something that was already written perfectly? I was very clear to my mum that I understood it just fine, so why wasn't that enough?

Multiple-choice questions always felt like a much easier way to demonstrate my understanding. I think that's because, for me, when I have clear options for the task, it all just clicks. It's much more obvious what I'm being asked to do. What I've come to understand is that clarity and context aren't just helpful for me; they're essential.

When something makes sense in a real-world way, I'm far more likely to engage with it, learn from it, and feel confident doing it. It's not about being difficult or resistant; it's about needing experiences to be meaningful. And when that happens, everything just clicks.

~ A page for your thoughts ~

MENTAL HEALTH & SELF-CARE

Autism Spectrum Disorder isn't a mental health issue; it's a neurological difference. I feel strongly that this distinction needs to be talked about more. Personally, I don't struggle much with mental health issues, and I believe there are reasons for that.

When I read parents' comments on my Facebook page about their children facing situations that I know would have severely impacted my own mental health, I completely understand why mental health struggles are so common. For me, the real issue isn't my autism by itself; it's the way the world responds to it. A lack of understanding, especially in schools and the wider community, creates environments that are overwhelming, distressing, and sometimes even harmful. This isn't just frustrating; it's awful – because it's preventable.

I want to advocate for parents who see their children struggling but aren't being heard. Too often, their concerns are dismissed, leaving both parents and children feeling invalidated and unsupported. As someone who didn't go to school, I don't know for sure how I would have found it. I know not all schools are the same, but they are supposed to be places where all children can thrive.

Yet many autistic students are placed in situations that fail to accommodate their needs. I'm sure that if I'd been forced into some of those situations myself, it would have taken a serious toll on my mental health. Being forced to wear certain clothing, interacting with peers in games or lessons when I want to focus on my own learning or maintain my personal space, being asked to speak up in front of everyone when I feel unsafe, or being forced to cope in loud environments were all experiences that would have been extremely difficult for me.

I've had messages from many teachers who genuinely care about their students and want to see them succeed. But they, too, are being failed by a system that doesn't give them the support, resources, or flexibility to make real change. The problem isn't just within individual classrooms; it's the structure of the education system itself.

I often wonder whether it would make more sense to support children in their special interests and help them develop valuable life skills. These are skills that could lead to fulfilling careers, whether employed or self-employed, instead of forcing them through a curriculum filled with subjects they have no interest in and may never use. I was fortunate to be aware of my diagnosis from a young age, which helped me understand myself rather than judge myself unfairly.

I learned to challenge myself within my capabilities, not to push beyond my limits or compare myself to others. That gave me confidence. My brother, for example, couldn't read until he was ten years old, but that didn't stop him from learning. He just needed more time. Now, you could put him next to anyone his age, and his reading skills would be the same. You'd never know he'd struggled for so long.

Not learning something at the same time as others doesn't mean you'll never get it. It's like building a puzzle: some of us just take longer to find the right pieces, but the picture still comes together. I haven't been forced to prove my learning through exams or tests. Instead, I've been encouraged to apply what

I've learned in my own time and at my own pace. That has given me confidence in my ability to do better. However, I also know how easy it is to spiral.

According to Autistica, autistic people in the UK make up approximately 1% of the population, yet we account for 11% of all suicides. The Office for National Statistics (2021) reported that the overall suicide rate was 10.5 per 100,000 for men compared to 5.5 for women.

To keep myself on track, I set small goals throughout the day. I actively try to maintain a positive mindset, which isn't always easy and sometimes feels impossible, but it helps keep frustration and anxiety from taking over.

When I'm faced with a problem, I've learned to take a step back and focus on finding a solution, even though controlling my emotions can still be difficult. I try to shift my mindset from 'This is overwhelming' to 'This is frustrating, but how am I going to deal with it?' It's not easy, especially if I'm already struggling, but it helps me avoid anxiety attacks or shutdowns.

I've heard that it's impossible to be both logical and emotional at the same time. If that's true, then tricking my brain into 'logical mode' makes it easier to process what's upsetting me. I wonder if this is why some of us are accused of being robot-like or uncaring, when, in reality, I've identified an emotional difficulty and instinctively shifted into logical mode as a coping mechanism.

It's also interesting how many people still believe that autistic individuals lack empathy. From what I've experienced with my own family, neurodivergent friends, and even within myself, the opposite is often true. I feel too much empathy, to the point where it becomes overwhelming. And when that happens to me, I feel like my subconscious throws me into logical thinking as a form of self-protection.

When I find myself facing an overwhelming problem or I'm unable to deal with a sensory situation, it's crucial for me to give myself time to think. If needed, I take myself physically away from the situation; otherwise, my brain shuts down completely.

Finding What Works for Me

I've always stayed clear of medication because I had bad side effects when I was younger, and it put me off completely. I've always struggled with sleep, but I later found out about melatonin.

I take 1mg melatonin about 30 minutes before I go to bed and stay off all technology. If I do that, I usually drift off to sleep. However, if I take some melatonin and stay on my phone or watch television, my brain gets wired again. I end up wide awake and then crash hard, which leaves me feeling exhausted the next day.

I've been lucky in many ways: knowing my diagnosis early, having the space to learn at my own pace, and being supported by people who understand me. But I know not everyone gets that. I've seen how easily experiences can spiral when needs aren't met and how damaging it can be when people are forced to fit into systems that don't make room for difference.

I often think about how different experiences might have been if I hadn't had that support. It's made me realise how important it is to listen, to adapt, and to create environments where people aren't punished for being different.

MENTAL HEALTH & SELF-CARE

Stepping Outside My Comfort Zone

In my first book, I talked about how scary flying was for me, not just the flight itself, but everything around it. From a sensory point of view, the sounds, the queues, and not knowing what to expect made it really stressful.

Even though my mum had been practically begging my brother and me to go abroad, we always said no. We went abroad on holiday twice when I was little. The first time, my mum took us to stay with family in Sweden for a week. I remember that being fun because it felt like a home away from home.

Although it was different, it somehow felt familiar to us. Maybe that was because we were so little. I was six, and my brother was three, and we enjoyed our time visiting museums and exploring the forests. However, when we travelled to Gran Canaria a few years later, we stayed in a holiday apartment, and it didn't feel safe. It felt empty and lifeless. I remember my brother and I asking my mum the night we arrived how many sleeps it would be until we could go home, and we kept asking until we left.

When we were younger, Mum always brought our own bedding or sheets whenever we stayed away from home. That helped with sensory issues like strong smells or uncomfortable textures, and it made a big difference. But being in a new country without all the other comforts we were familiar with caused my brother and me a lot of stress.

We didn't know where to go or where to eat, and after being on a plane, we knew we were far away from home, which added to our anxiety. Mum did her best. We spent a lot of time in the apartment playing board games, but it must have been obvious to her that we weren't happy, because that was the last time we flew abroad as children. To get a break without leaving the country, Mum tried taking us to a caravan park in England when I was twelve. That turned into a nightmare. My brother and I really struggled because we didn't see the point of being away from home. Swimming in a different pool and not having that familiarity made us feel trapped and anxious.

It was anything but enjoyable, especially as my brother was prone to severe meltdowns and could be inconsolable for hours. When Mum realised nothing was going to make us enjoy ourselves, she decided to leave early and took us home.

Looking back now, I feel bad for her. She was trying to take us somewhere new, but we just didn't want to be there. It wasn't that we didn't want to have fun; it was just really hard being away from our safe place. All we wanted was to be at home, where everything was familiar. Recently, we had to fly to Ireland for family reasons. The idea of flying out of the country made us really anxious. But strangely, when we booked the flights, I felt excited about going. Maybe because this wasn't a holiday, it was something we had to do, and I felt more relaxed. If it had been a trip just for us, we probably would have kept delaying it. But since it was essential, it fell out of my hands, which made it easier for me.

My brother's biggest challenge was being away from his support dog. He relies on that security, so being away for three nights was tough.

We flew with a budget airline and kept things simple by taking only carry-on luggage. Since we were only staying a few days, that was enough. I packed my phone, charger, a book, headphones, a sunflower lanyard, three sets of clothes, and a small toiletries bag. This time, because we were only travelling with carry-on luggage, we just packed pillowcases from home to use at the hotel instead of duvets and towels. We arrived at the airport two hours early. It wasn't as busy as I expected, so we went straight to security. But when I got to the gate, I felt confused. Everyone else around me seemed to know exactly what to do, and I struggled to keep up.

Feeling rushed, I emptied my pockets, placed my bag, shoes, and jacket into the tray, and was shown to the X-ray scanner. I hated it because instead of just walking through, I was expected to know what to do. They kept telling me I had my arms in the wrong position, and it was embarrassing and stressful because I didn't feel they communicated what they wanted very well. I expect that as a young adult, they assumed I'd done it before.

Once I collected my things, I felt relieved, but then I had too much time to overthink the flight. We sat in a quiet restaurant, but I couldn't eat anything. When I'm anxious, it feels like a fluttering in my stomach, and it stays like that until I complete whatever it is I'm preparing for, in this case, waiting to board the plane.

When our gate was called, we showed our boarding passes and passports then entered the tunnel to enter the plane. We'd been waiting in line for around twenty minutes when the staff told us all to go back to the gate because they were changing planes. That didn't help my anxiety at all. In that moment, I just wanted to leave the airport and go home. I wondered if it was a sign not to get on the plane at all and started thinking about all the reasons not to go.

But I was determined to get to Dublin, so we walked to the new gate. I kept telling myself: it's only an hour and twenty-minute flight; I didn't have long to endure it. A bus took us to the plane, and as I walked up the steps into the aircraft, I felt a sense of relief. In my head, I was already in Ireland because at that point, it felt like there was no turning back. My mum has always been afraid of flying. She struggles with the g-forces during take-off and turns, something my brother actually enjoyed.

I didn't like the feeling either, especially since it was a night flight and pitch-black outside. When the plane tilted or descended, I couldn't see the ground, which made it feel like we were falling out of the sky. Luckily, being a short flight, it felt like we'd only just taken off when they told us to prepare for landing.

Arriving in Ireland gave me a real boost of confidence, and it wasn't just temporary. As silly as it may sound to some, I think it's because I felt like I escaped the jaws of death.

I also want to say thank you to everyone on my Facebook page who offered advice and encouragement. Reading your messages at the airport helped me feel more confident. You were all so kind! On the way back, we paid extra and flew with a different airline. The difference was amazing. We all felt much more comfortable, and I'm so glad we made that decision because it has given us more confidence to think about flying again in the future.

If you aren't scared to fly, it probably wouldn't make any difference, but the seats felt more comfortable, which helps when there's turbulence, and it was much quieter inside. If you fear flying, I think it's worth the extra cost to make the experience easier.

Flying used to feel impossible, something I'd avoid at all costs. But this trip showed me that with the right preparation, support, and mindset, I can do difficult things.

It didn't erase the anxiety or make everything easy, but it reminded me that I'm capable of more than I sometimes give myself credit for. I still prefer the comfort of home, and I probably always will, but now I know that stepping outside my comfort zone doesn't have to mean losing my sense of safety. It just means finding new ways to carry it with me.

~ A page for your thoughts ~

FACING LIFE CHANGES

My Nan passed away in 2022, and that was the first time I had ever lost someone really close to me. She had dementia for several years, so while her passing wasn't unexpected, it was still very difficult.

When I was younger, I was very close to her and visited her most weekends. But as her dementia progressed, she gradually forgot who my brother and I were.

By the late stages of her illness, I felt disconnected from her. She was no longer the person I had known growing up. It was like she had become a shell of who she once was. She looked the same, but her personality was completely different. The hardest part was watching my grandad have to cope with it as well.

Her funeral was not only my first time attending a funeral, but also the first time I had ever been fitted for and worn a suit. When my family and I went to get suits, my grandad chose the colour scheme and design himself. That made the experience easier for me, as we were simply measured one by one and handed a suit to try on. I liked that I didn't have to make any decisions myself.

When it was my turn to try on the suit, I wasn't sure about it. I didn't like the way it fit. I asked if it was supposed to feel tight around my chest and arms, and I was told it fit correctly. I figured that since I'd only be wearing it for half a day, I would be okay with it. But it did make me think about how difficult it must be for children at school with sensory issues to wear a uniform, or for people who have to wear one every day for work. I couldn't imagine having to wear that suit all the time. We were only hiring them for the week, so at least I didn't have to worry about keeping it.

On the day of the funeral, I was asked if I wanted to travel with my dad, grandad, and aunt in the limo behind the hearse. The thought of that was uncomfortable and too much for me, so I chose to drive my mum and brother instead. Driving helps me relax. When I'm driving, I become so focused that my brain doesn't have an opportunity to overthink.

Before the funeral, my brother and I were asked if we wanted to help carry the coffin alongside our dad and uncle. My brother really wanted to do it, but he said he would only feel comfortable if I were carrying it with him. I told him I couldn't commit because I didn't know how I'd feel on the day. When the moment came, I did end up helping to carry the coffin into the church. It was difficult, but I was proud of myself for doing it. I knew how much it meant to my brother that I was there with him, and I knew it meant a lot to my grandad too.

After the funeral, I understood why my mum had protected my brother and me from attending funerals in the past. I found it extremely distressing and emotionally challenging. It didn't bring me the sense of closure that people often say funerals are for, and it was hard to see my family upset.

Since then, I've said that in the future, when there's a funeral, I'd rather not attend. It's not because I don't care; it's because I care so much that it's too emotionally difficult for me to put myself through it. It's easier for me to come to terms with loss in my own time and my own way.

~ A page for your thoughts ~

LEARNING TO DRIVE

This is the part where I talk about cars. A lot. Possibly more than anyone asked for. But when something becomes a special interest, it's not just a hobby. For me, it's a language, a comfort, and a way of making sense of the world.

As I mentioned in *The Secrets of My Spectrum*, cars have been my obsession for as long as I can remember. When I was little, I had boxes of toy cars and a car mat I loved playing on. For me, everything had to be as realistic as possible. I would sit and play with my cars for hours in my own world, creating traffic scenarios and strictly following 'real' road rules with the markings on the mat. In the summer, I would create my own roads outside on the garden pavement with coloured chalk. I loved making large road networks with car parks, roundabouts, and houses.

I'd even organise traffic jams on purpose, just to figure out how to clear them. I wasn't just playing; I was problem-solving. Every car had a purpose, every road had a rule, and I could spend hours fine-tuning the layout until it felt just right. Looking back, I think it was one of the first ways I found comfort in structure and logic. That's probably why cars made so much sense to me from the start. Unlike people, cars followed simple rules.

They move in predictable ways, respond to clear instructions, and operate within systems that are designed to be logical. There's a structure to it all: speed limits, road markings, indicators, road signs, and once I understood those rules, everything just clicked. I didn't have to guess what a car was thinking or worry about hidden meanings. It was all laid out, step by step. For someone like me, who finds comfort in clarity and consistency, cars weren't just interesting; they were understandable.

As I grew up, I transitioned into playing racing games such as *Gran Turismo* and *Test Drive Unlimited*. I remember how amazed I was the first time I played them. Even in the virtual world, I would end up abiding by road laws, following traffic, sticking to speed limits, and waiting at traffic lights.

It wasn't about racing. I didn't care about winning or crashing through barriers. I was quite happy listening to the game's soundtracks and spending hours cruising around the virtual map. It gave me a sense of control and calm.

When I was 13, I got a Logitech G29 racing wheel and gearbox for Christmas. This was my first time using a realistic setup for the games I loved. Thanks to the realism in modern games like *Gran Turismo* and *Euro Truck Simulator 2*, they helped me learn a lot of driving fundamentals.

It might sound surprising, but practising things like reversing trailers in *Euro Truck Simulator 2* and racing hundreds of different cars on tracks in *Gran Turismo* with the steering wheel, gearbox, and pedals gave me skills I could transfer to real-world driving.

I knew about things such as how front-wheel-drive cars are more prone to understeer, while rear-wheel-drive cars tend to oversteer. But being able to feel the difference through the wheel made it so much easier to understand.

I would even challenge myself by turning off driving assists like traction control and ABS. That taught me the importance of car

LEARNING TO DRIVE

control, how to fine-tune my throttle and braking inputs, and how to respect a car's limitations. That's something I wouldn't have fully understood without those games. It's something I actively think about when I'm driving out on the road now.

The following year, I was given Admiral Young Driver lessons for Christmas, and to say I was excited is an understatement. It's a scheme that allows you to start learning to drive off-road with an instructor.

The lessons take place in large car parks with roundabouts and parking bays where you share the space with other young learners. My first lesson was in a city, on the rooftop of a multi-storey car park, which was unexpected but fun.

I remember feeling both nervous and excited. After waiting in line with my mum, I was assigned an instructor. As we walked over to his car, he asked if I'd had any experience before and how much I knew about driving. I told him it was my first time, but I was really into cars and used a simulator at home. He said, 'You should get used to this quite quickly, then.' And so, my first lesson began.

I climbed into the driver's seat while he explained the basics to me: mirrors, pedals, gears, and buttons. Once he was finished, he told me I could start the car. My anxiety was through the roof, and my left leg was shaking like crazy. I explained to my instructor that I'm autistic and that my leg shakes when I'm nervous. He was really understanding and told me to start whenever I was ready.

After about four minutes of chatting about cars, I calmed down enough to get going. The lesson was really enjoyable, and looking back, I think those early Young Driver lessons were what first sparked my interest in becoming a driving instructor myself. If you've read my first book, you'll know when I turned sixteen. My mum encouraged me to get a 50cc motorbike. She wanted me to gain some confidence and have some independence in being able to get around.

At first, I wasn't interested because I thought motorbikes were too dangerous. But after talking it through and doing some research, I found out it could only reach 30 mph, and I'd just be riding locally, not far from home. So I decided to buy one and take my CBT, which gave me some early road experience.

For the first few times I took it out, I had my mum follow me until I felt comfortable. I had that motorcycle for a year before I got my car and sold it. During that time, I was really glad I'd had it. She was right, it was a great confidence builder for me.

I remember the day I was officially able to drive my mum's car on the road. I was sitting in the kitchen, staring up at the clock, waiting for the insurance policy we'd bought earlier that day to kick in so I could go out and start driving. I walked up to the car and jumped into the driver's seat with my mum in the passenger seat next to me. I was both nervous and excited, but once I started driving, I was locked in and adapted quickly.

I'd downloaded the DVLA theory test app onto my phone a year earlier, so I was already familiar with the Highway Code. The app was amazing because it was essentially like taking mock theory tests over and over again. With so many different questions, it was a great way for me to practise until I felt confident enough to take the real test.

The year spent riding my motorbike had already given me a lot of experience. From that day on, my mum made me drive everywhere we went to build up my confidence and gain more experience on the road. I went

out with her often to practise manoeuvres and build my confidence behind the wheel.
I wanted to make sure that by the time my practical test came around, I was as ready and as comfortable as I could be to help ease my anxiety. I also watched lots of driving instructor videos online to get an idea of what to expect on the day.

Taking My Theory Test

When I arrived at the theory test centre, I felt very anxious and didn't know what to expect. I found out I had to go into a large waiting room by myself because family weren't allowed in. Once inside, I walked up to the counter, where a man was waiting. I showed him my licence and was told to put my belongings into a locker.

I then entered a room full of computers where others were taking their tests. Sitting down in my booth felt a bit odd. The computer and software looked really outdated, like something straight out of the early 2000s, especially compared to the sleek, modern app I'd been using on my phone for months.

That unexpected change really threw me off. Once I'd completed the test, I had no idea if I'd passed. I collected my belongings from the locker, and the man at the counter handed me a piece of paper before sitting back down. I stood there, unsure what to do, until he said, 'That's it, you can go.'

As I stepped outside the room, my mum was waiting expectantly. The moment she saw me, she asked if I'd passed. I hesitated, unsure, until she gently reminded me to check the paper. My heart pounded as I unfolded it. I'd passed! A wave of joy rushed through me, and I couldn't stop smiling.

LEARNING TO DRIVE

Practical Driving Test

Now that I'd passed my theory test, my mum called a driving school to arrange a lesson and assess how test-ready I was. On the day the instructor was coming, I felt nervous and found myself overthinking. My brain went into overdrive, running through every possible scenario.

What if I misunderstood an instruction or didn't know how to respond fast enough? I wasn't worried about the driving itself; I was worried about the social part.
Would the instructor expect small talk? The unpredictable nature of human interaction is where things get complicated for me.

When he arrived, he was very friendly. After a bit of chatting, we walked up to his car, and he showed me where everything was inside his learner car. Once I was happy with the controls, he told me I could start when I was ready. Just like my very first Young Driver lesson, my leg was shaking so much from nerves that I couldn't begin.

My mum had already told him I was autistic, so I explained that my leg shakes when I'm anxious but calms down after a moment. He was friendly and understanding, and after a minute, I was able to start driving. His car was quite different from ours, which made me uncomfortable. I'd already spent so many hours driving our car that it felt second nature, and I knew exactly where everything was. I made a few mistakes, but as the lesson went on, I became more comfortable with his car. We drove around town and practised parking manoeuvres to assess my skill level. It was easy to talk to him since we mostly chatted about cars.

At the end of the lesson, he told me I was ready for my test, which really surprised me. Apart from my Young Driver sessions a year earlier, I hadn't had any formal lessons on the road. But all the time I had spent practising with my mum, plus a year riding my motorbike and working on manoeuvres, had been enough.

I'm not saying this to boast, but to show that when you have a special interest and the right support, you can reach your goals quickly through determination and focus. Those early Young Driver lessons gave me a solid foundation, and everything since – riding my motorbike on the road, driving my mum's car, and watching loads of driving instructor videos online, helped get me test-ready within a couple of months.

The evening before my driving test, my instructor texted my mum to say he was ill and couldn't take me to the test centre the next morning. Oddly, this turned out to be great news because after a bit of research, it meant I could actually use our own car. That was going to be a lot easier since I was already so comfortable driving it. On the day of my test, my mum kept reassuring me that if I didn't pass, I could always retake it. But I was desperate to become an independent driver, so I had built up the need to pass in my head and was really hyped up about it.

When I arrived at the test centre, I was shaky and nervous. As soon as I started our car, I stopped shaking and became hyper-focused, blocking out my anxiety. My logical mind kicked in, and I put everything I'd learned from the videos I watched and from driving with my mum into practice.

I was so well prepared that I actually enjoyed the test. During the test, I did go the wrong way at one point, but I knew from my research that as long as you keep driving safely and make your way back onto the test route, it isn't a failure. If anything, I thought it was a good thing because I was able to show that I could safely make my way back onto the correct route at the next roundabout. When we returned to the test centre, the examiner asked if I was happy with my drive.

I said yes, I thought I did fine, and then he started typing on his iPad. I wasn't sure if I'd passed because there was a short silence, but when he asked for my driving licence, I realised he was filling out my pass certificate. I was so proud of myself. Being able to drive unlocked a lot for me. It meant I could visit family far away and go anywhere I wanted, which gave me a substantial confidence boost I didn't even realise I needed.

Having this level of independence and freedom really changed my life, and some of my major anxieties started to fade. For example, I used to hate traffic jams because I felt trapped, but now, when I'm driving, and we get stuck in traffic, it doesn't seem to be a problem anymore. I'm not sure why, but it barely affects me now. It's funny how autism affects me. I could drive all the way to Scotland, literally the other end of the country, without a second thought. But ask me to call and book a hotel? Not happening. And if I'd booked one online, then turned up and had to press a buzzer to speak to someone just to get in? Then guess who's sleeping in his car!

The worst part is that I likely wouldn't even get my money back. How would I? I'm not about to phone up and ask for a refund when the reason I didn't stay is that I didn't want to talk to anyone in the first place.

For anyone who feels anxious about learning to drive or doubts whether they are capable, I want to share my younger brother's experience, with his permission. Some people assumed he was 'too autistic' or 'too PDA' (Pathological Demand Avoidance) to manage driving lessons. But we encouraged him to give it a try as soon as he was old enough, to help give him the confidence that I'd found.

LEARNING TO DRIVE

To help ease his anxiety, I sat in on his lessons with the instructor, quietly in the back seat, so he knew I was there if he needed reassurance. His first instructor was a little too laid-back for him, so my mum did some phoning around. She got chatting to a lady who said that her husband is autistic and also an instructor, so Mum quickly booked lessons with him. This instructor was amazing and a perfect fit for my brother. I wasn't needed during his lessons very quickly after that. With the right support, we can achieve far more than we often give ourselves credit for.

My brother passed his driving test on his first attempt, which made a huge difference to his confidence too. Now he is a confident and competent driver. Not every instructor suits every learner, so don't feel bad if you need to try a different approach. Finding an instructor and environment you feel comfortable in is the key.

MORE SECRETS OF MY SPECTRUM

My First Car

I was excited about buying my first car. I only considered dealerships because dealing with a private individual felt too overwhelming for me. I don't feel comfortable looking around someone else's car while they are standing there watching me, and I don't think I can be as thorough in my inspection as I would like to be because I feel awkward. It was much easier for me to use a dealership. Since it isn't their personal vehicle, I feel I can speak more freely, even if it means paying a bit more than I would buying privately.

Something I hate is haggling over the price of a vehicle, or anything for that matter. When I'm looking to buy something, the price on the listing is the price I'll pay. If I think it's too much, I'll look elsewhere. I value transparency, and when prices feel like a negotiation trap, it puts me on edge. I don't want to play psychological chess with someone or pretend I'm comfortable bartering when I'm not. I just want clarity. Is this car worth the asking price to me, or not? That is the decision I make.

After finding a car I really liked within my price range at a dealership, my mum handled the communication side of things for me. When we went to see it, I took my time looking it over, and we went for a test drive. I'd already run an online history check to make sure everything was clean, and having Mum help with the communication side made the whole experience far less stressful. For me, that made all the difference. I paid the asking price because I loved the car and knew it was the one I wanted.

Driving it home for the first time felt brilliant. It isn't flashy or brand new – it's an old estate car, but it's mine. I chose it, checked it, paid for it, and now I was behind the wheel. That was a special moment.

~ A page for your thoughts ~

HANDLING THE UNEXPECTED

One day, while I was driving home, a police car was stationed at the bottom of the road, and a row of traffic cones had been set up, blocking access to the street my house is on. I was sat there for a moment at a red light, trying to process what was happening, and realised I was going to have to make a decision. Either pull over and speak to the police to find out if I could get through to my driveway, or park somewhere else and walk the rest of the way home.

I decided that as soon as the light turned green, I would drive up to the officer and explain that I lived on that street, hoping they would let me through. I started to say I lived down this road, and luckily, I barely had time to finish my sentence when the officer gave me a quick nod and said, 'Okay, wait there for a second, and I'll move these cones out of your way.' He shifted the cones and repositioned his car just enough for me to drive through.

It turned out that a bus had broken down further up the road and had spilt oil everywhere, so they had closed the road until it was cleaned up. Since I was having a good day and feeling confident, I handled the situation without any issues.

But I know that if I'd been feeling overwhelmed or struggling that day, I would have avoided the interaction altogether and chosen the easier option, parking a street or two away and walking home instead. The surprise element of the situation forced me to react quickly without overthinking it, and

HANDLING THE UNEXPECTED

I've noticed that in moments like that, when a problem appears out of nowhere, I tend to manage better as long as I'm feeling okay in myself and don't have time to spiral into overanalysing it.

When I went to the post office to send a gift, I was asked to fill out a form, which caught me off guard. As soon as I began writing, my hand started shaking. It was a busy time, and knowing there were a lot of people waiting behind me made it worse. The pressure to write quickly and make sure I was getting it right, knowing I was holding up the queue, became overwhelming, and I ended up having an anxiety attack right there.

Although I'm getting much better at handling these kinds of situations, they can still feel challenging sometimes. Everyday tasks can still present challenges for me in ways that might not seem like a big deal to other people. A recent example was when I went to buy some silicone for a house project. Nothing out of the ordinary, just a simple purchase, but when I was paying for it the cashier asked me for ID, I felt a sudden wave of anxiety. Even though I knew I was old enough and had my ID with me, my heart rate still spiked as I pulled it out and handed it over. I don't know why these small interactions can make me feel so on edge, but I can't seem to control my reaction when it happens.

In hindsight, it may have been because I definitely wouldn't have thought I'd need my ID to buy silicone, so there was no preparation on my part to have any interaction other than to just smile and say thanks after buying it. There are certain unexpected situations that don't bother me as much as they used to.

I used to get really anxious if someone showed up at my house unannounced, but now most of the time I can handle it without too much stress. Knowing that my home is my safe space, where I can retreat if I need to, helps me feel more in control. I used to have an autism sign on the door to let people know I might not answer, and while I still have it, I no longer rely on it as much.

Instead, I installed a CCTV system that allows me to check who is at the door from my phone, which has made a huge difference. I'm happy to answer for deliveries, but if I see someone with a clipboard or someone I'm not expecting, I just ignore them. It's a simple solution that gives me peace of mind.

The only time I felt really thrown off was when the police showed up at my door one night. I couldn't make out who was outside at first, and when I opened the door to see uniformed officers standing there, I felt a rush of nervousness and confusion. It wasn't the fact that they were police. My mum used to work for the police, and we have family friends who were officers. It was the unexpected nature of their visit that caught me off guard. They quickly explained that they were searching for a missing vulnerable person who had been seen walking in our area, and they asked if our CCTV had picked up any relevant footage. After checking, I was able to confirm that the person had passed by our house. Although the whole experience was a little nerve-racking, I felt good about being able to help.

Even something as simple as online shopping has its own set of challenges for me. I once ordered an appliance that was advertised with next-day delivery, only to find out after I'd already paid that a third-party delivery service was handling it and they wouldn't be able to deliver for another two weeks.

I was frustrated because I chose that specific appliance for the next-day delivery, so I decided to cancel my order. But instead of offering an easy online cancellation, the company required me to call their helpline. At that moment, the idea of making that phone call felt completely overwhelming, and I ended up avoiding it altogether. I let my family deal with the cancellation for me instead.

Experiences like this knock my confidence when it comes to buying things online, because they add an extra layer of uncertainty and stress, experiences most people wouldn't even think twice about. At the end of the day, I know that these little challenges will always be part of my life, and although they're still a struggle, I'm learning to navigate them better over time.

As I've said before, some days I handle unexpected situations easily. Other days, they feel like a mountain to climb. But either way, I'll figure them out eventually.

~ A page for your thoughts ~

LEARNING SELF-ADVOCACY

I've always found it difficult to speak up for myself, and when I was younger, I'd quite happily let my mum do the talking on my behalf because I struggled to communicate, especially with people I didn't know well, and even more so with complete strangers.

Now that I'm older and out more on my own, handling these situations myself isn't always easy, and I often find myself relying on masking.

I find it hard to say no. My default response is to agree without stopping to think it through or checking whether I can actually fulfil the request, simply to avoid seeming rude, mean, or selfish. I hate confrontation. I've always been the person who avoids causing a fuss, either because it feels uncomfortable or because I'm too anxious to push back.

I once paid a cashier with a £20 note for an item that cost £12, but they only gave me £6 change instead of £8. I noticed straight away, yet I stayed silent. I hadn't expected to be given the wrong amount of change, and the thought of correcting them made me too anxious. I remember walking back to my car thinking I should have said something, but by that point I was already accepting I wouldn't be getting my £2 back.

Looking back, I feel frustrated that I didn't stand up for myself. In those moments, I'm caught off guard and unprepared. If I'd anticipated it, or if I'd been having a more confident day, maybe I would have spoken up. But most of the time, I feel too intimidated to correct mistakes, even when I know I'm right. Now, at 21, I'm learning to advocate for myself. I've realised that it's okay to say no if I don't want to do something, and that I shouldn't feel bad putting myself first.

Putting myself first is not selfish – sometimes it is necessary. I don't have to feel guilty for looking out for myself and saying no to something I don't really want to do.

~ A page for your thoughts ~

FINDING CALM IN MY INTERESTS

My mum asked me recently if I thought my hobbies were actually ways I keep my anxiety at bay. It struck me as a really interesting question. I don't consciously set out to avoid anxiety when I'm doing these things, but after reflecting on it, I wonder if they might be a subconscious way of helping me manage it, an almost self regulation I didn't realise I was practising.

When I'm absorbed in a hobby or lost in an interest, everything else seems to fade into the background. The noise of the day quiets down, and I can focus on something that feels safe and predictable. If I'm anxious or heading towards a shutdown, immersing myself in these activities is often the lifeline that pulls me back. It's not about distraction so much as creating a pocket of calm where my mind can breathe.

Sometimes it's the rhythm of the task, the repetitive motions, the familiar steps, that soothes me. Other times it's the satisfaction of seeing progress, whether that's editing a video, a completed car detail, or even just a tidy space. These small victories remind me that I can create order and clarity, even when my thoughts feel chaotic.

Music plays a massive role in my life. It helps me in so many different ways, and depending on how I'm feeling, my music preferences can change every day. I have hundreds of playlists on my phone, and I pick songs based on the emotions they stir in me. Whether they make me feel empowered and confident or calm me down with soothing instrumentals, music is something I would really struggle without. It's a mood regulator, and it helps me stay focused. When I need to get things done, listening to the right kind of music keeps my mind from wandering off or getting distracted by outside noise.

I've written most of this book with music playing in the background. Not all music has the same effect, though. For example, my brother loves heavy metal, and while some days I can tolerate it, other days it feels like the beats are vibrating through my head, and it sends me into sensory overload. If I'm already feeling overwhelmed, it can easily push me into a shutdown.

Since I got my car, I started learning how to maintain it myself, and I discovered car detailing videos and became completely hooked. It was so satisfying to watch, and I started to learn how to detail my car myself. I went and bought some equipment and products, and now detailing my car has become one of my favourite things to do. I often spend hours each week cleaning it because it's incredibly therapeutic and helps me centre myself. Even in the depths of winter, when it's freezing outside, I'm out there scrubbing away while the neighbours probably wonder if I've finally lost the plot.

Car maintenance is just as important to me as keeping it clean. One Christmas, my mum bought me a maintenance logbook to track everything I'd done, and I absolutely loved it.

The book includes weekly checks, and there's something deeply satisfying about ticking off each entry and knowing I'm staying ahead of potential problems.

I enjoy keeping on top of things to reduce the chances of unexpected breakdowns, and I get a real sense of achievement from doing the work myself whenever I can. Photography is another hobby I've really come to love. I often take my camera with me when I'm walking the dog or going on day trips. It gives me a creative outlet to clear my mind, and I enjoy capturing different perspectives through the lens. Whether it is landscapes, cars, or everyday moments, photography helps me stay grounded and focused in the present.

I enjoy playing the piano because it can be soft and calming one moment, and heavy and dramatic the next. I struggled to learn to read music, and even now it all looks like hieroglyphics to me, maybe it's because of my dyslexia. I would get really frustrated trying to remember notes and lose interest quickly. Then everything changed when I found piano tutorials online.

They show a line and the note's letter coming up. Combined with a note overlay I bought for my piano to put over the keys, I was able to play and have since found it much easier to learn. It's not the way I was supposed to learn, but it worked very well for me. Even so, I do struggle to finish songs. I'll start one, but then get distracted by another tune I want to try, so I end up switching halfway through.

As a result, I know the beginning of a lot of songs but rarely finish them. But one song was different. I made sure to learn it all the way through because my mum really liked it.

Over the last couple of years, I've started going to car shows, and they have quickly become one of my favourite things to do. I really enjoy walking around, admiring all the different cars, and taking photos.

Being at these events helps me develop my social skills, too. I find it much easier to talk to people when the conversation is about cars. It's so much easier to chat with someone when I already know a lot about the topic.

~ A page for your thoughts ~

WHY I CAN ONE DAY & NOT THE NEXT

If I'm having a confident day, I might try something new. You may be thinking: how can I do it one day but not the next? Let me try to explain. Something I was told growing up is that when you've done something once, it gets easier the second time because it's no longer new. You've already had that experience, and you can build on it with a better idea of what to expect the next time.

But expectations don't always pan out the way I think they will. Events don't always go the same way every time, which I've found is all part of the learning process. I try my best because that's all I can do. My best one day might not look the same as my best on another. One day, I can pick up the phone to speak to a family member, and yet on another day, I can feel completely incapable of doing the same thing.

This is strange for people around me who don't understand, because in their minds, I'm fully capable. They've seen me do it before, so why on this occasion am I physically shaking and feeling debilitated by the thought of it? I wish I could tell you why this happens to me, but I'm still struggling to understand it myself. It isn't something that makes logical sense to me either.

The best way I can think of to explain this is to imagine asking a professional darts player: 'Why can't you hit a bullseye every time? You've done it several times before, so you know how to do it. Why do you sometimes miss?' That is how autism feels to me. Sometimes, all the challenges and external or environmental factors come together in perfect harmony, and I feel confident and able to push myself. However, I never know when that will be, so I can't prepare or plan ahead for it.

From a young age, I've always sought to fix problems and find solutions. I find that I can often do things for others that I wouldn't be able to do for myself, like going to a pharmacy to get over-the-counter medicine. This would usually terrify me if I needed it for myself, but when my mum was ill and needed my help, that gave me more confidence to try.

I'm not sure why I struggle to do these things for myself. This is hard to explain, because if I've gone out to get something for my brother and then later claim I can't do it for myself, how strange does that look? I've come to the conclusion that I tend to overthink what I'm going to be asked. Am I going to have to fill out paperwork or stand in a long queue? When I'm doing it for someone else, it's harder to think about my own needs because I'm too busy thinking about theirs.

On those confident days, I still encourage myself to try new things I wouldn't usually feel comfortable doing, or that I tend to avoid. I set myself goals, nothing too big, just ones I could accomplish but might not particularly enjoy, such as asking where something is in a shop, making a quick phone call, or writing and replying to a more complicated email.

Since becoming self-employed, I've received numerous emails, and this task has become much easier for me now. So I can say that with experience comes more confidence, but also that autism is always the boss, and I'm not in control of my abilities all the time. Now that I'm older, I've realised that becoming an adult is a process. You don't just wake up one day and suddenly know how to deal with every unexpected event that pops up. It happens gradually, over time and with experience.

It doesn't occur in the same timeframe for everyone, and we all reach different stages at different times. I remind myself not to judge my abilities against others but on whether I'm progressing myself.

As a teenager, knowing that I couldn't rely on exam results, I hoped to become self-employed one day, but I wasn't sure how I would get there. It isn't easy, but I've had a lot of help, and with certain accommodations, I'm able to work successfully and learn what I need to make a living for myself.

With my diagnosis, I've learned more about the possible challenges I may face in the future so that I can seek out the help and accommodations I need early on. I'm glad that I was able to see my life and my capabilities with a realistic lens, so that I could learn gradually at my own pace and not feel pressured to live up to unfair expectations.

~ A page for your thoughts ~

EDUCATION

The years between sixteen and twenty-one were when everything changed for me. Not because I suddenly fit the system, but because I learned how to build my own way through it. I stopped trying to force myself into spaces that were not designed for me and started shaping my own path instead.

I know I was incredibly lucky that my mum was able and willing to home-educate me. That support gave me the breathing room to grow without constant pressure or comparison. I feel deeply privileged that I didn't have to face the daily overwhelm that so many neurodivergent students face. Things I know other kids like me find impossible to cope with, I didn't have to sit in noisy classrooms or navigate confusing social hierarchies just to get through the day. That space gave me the chance to grow in ways that felt safe and sustainable. Home education gave me the chance to learn in a way that worked for me. I could go at my own pace, dive deep into subjects I cared about, and nothing disrupted me or made my learning difficult.

I remember studying for my English IGCSE. I worked hard to complete the workbooks and proudly showed them to my mum, only to be told I had misunderstood the questions and my answers were wrong. It knocked my confidence. When I first learned grammar as a child, I had no problems because there were clear rules to follow.

But later English became less about rules and more about interpreting what was written between the lines and analysing writers' motives. I found that difficult, frustrating, and honestly pointless. I still do. Workbooks did not work for me. I needed a lot of help from my mum to fully understand what I was reading. They were too static.

Once my mum found video-based learning, everything became much easier. I absorb information visually, and once I had that visual element to link the text to, I could finally focus and understand subjects better. It wasn't perfect, but it helped a lot. It also made me realise how much learning depends on the method, not just the material. In schools, I imagine it is hard for teachers to meet every student's needs, especially when the system expects everyone to learn the same way.

I found out that exams would not be accessible to me after my mum spent a long time going around in circles trying to find an exam centre that could support my needs. I needed to use a computer instead of writing by hand because I type quickly but write slowly, and after a while, my handwriting gets smaller and harder to read. It would be considered unreadable after around twenty minutes. I also needed help understanding questions that were not worded in a way that made sense to me. Sitting still for long periods of time is tough. I stim a lot when I try to sit still, and my brain completely blanks under pressure, which makes it even harder to concentrate within a time limit.

I even spoke to my GP about possible medications, but all they ever did was make me fatigued. I definitely could not concentrate after taking them, so I threw them away and decided it was much better to work with my body and find workarounds than to work against myself.

My mum kept getting bounced from one person to another until, eventually, we were told it was not possible for me to get help without paperwork. As I was home-educated, that was impossible. With my autism diagnosis, I was told that because I was not at school, I could not access any help. So I focused on learning what interested me rather than chasing qualifications.

When COVID came along, the local college let me take an entrance test online instead of worrying about exams, which helped me so much. It was still timed, but because I was at home in a comfortable environment, I could start when I felt ready. I prepared myself with a glass of water and some music. When I got my results, I had achieved a Level 2 and I was over the moon. It meant I was ready to start A Levels.

However, when COVID continued, I felt it wasn't the right time to join a college for the first time. So, I convinced my mum that I could do just as well continuing to work online. I enrolled on an A-level psychology course alongside the design and video editing I was learning, which I found really interesting. Exams are not for everyone, and I don't think it is right that anyone should be locked out of further education simply because they do not want to pursue a formal maths or English qualification. While I understand the importance of those subjects in certain professions, many people face learning difficulties like dyscalculia or dyslexia, as well as neurodivergent challenges that make some lessons extremely frustrating.

Do we really need to dissect what Shakespeare was thinking when he wrote, or why a poet chose a particular word, in order to pursue any career? Struggling with maths does not mean someone cannot earn a good living, and struggling with English analysis does not mean someone cannot communicate effectively in their chosen career.

Instead of putting blocks in the way, why not inspire the next generation to discover their strengths and excel in those areas? Better to master what you can do well than be bogged down so much that you never have the opportunity to find out what that is. Qualifications should open doors, not slam them shut. Let us show our work in ways that make sense to our brains. Let us be measured by what we can do, not by how many boxes we tick. Let parents who work tirelessly to get their children learning in a way that suits them be trusted and supported.

A big turning point was when I realised the skills I had picked up using tools like Adobe weren't just useful skills, but they were doors to earning an income for myself. All at once, the hours I'd spent learning Photoshop, InDesign, Premiere Pro and other online applications weren't just hobbies; they were marketable skills. I could design posters, edit videos, or create layouts for people who needed them, and that opened up opportunities I hadn't considered before.

When I hyper-focus on something, I absorb a huge amount of knowledge and skill quickly. People often ask me, 'Where did you learn that?' and the truth is, I was interested in it and threw myself into it. Anxiety and timed exams stopped me from getting academic qualifications, but they never stopped me from learning and retaining what I had learned.

That said, I did need exact, step-by-step instructions for the software. If a tutorial said, 'click the settings icon', I needed to know exactly what that icon looked like and where it was on the screen. So, I learned to hunt down tutorials with clear visuals and follow along the steps to build real competence.
As I continue on my path, I know that the ability to adapt, self-teach, and dive deeply into my interests will always be one of my biggest strengths. I had at one point settled on the idea that I would become a driving instructor specialising in helping other autistic kids, but then...

EDUCATION

The Secrets of My Spectrum Changed Everything!

After I published my book, reviews slowly started to come in. People wrote to me about similar situations they had faced and thanked me for writing my book. I had parents tell me it helped them understand their children better, and I was over the moon.

It means a lot to me to think that my experiences could help someone else, because that was the reason I wanted to write the book in the first place. At first, I thought only friends and family would read it, but it grew into something much bigger than I'd ever expected.

I've had invites to go on the radio or visit schools, but I've always been too anxious about accepting them, it still terrifies me. I'm better now than I was, but I still don't feel ready for anything too public. Life in my twenties opened up more gradually. With supports in place, I could predict and prepare for things and push myself to feel more confident, but I'm still autistic, so I need to plan everything carefully.

When parents started asking me to write books for their younger children with illustrations, I looked for the perfect illustrator, and I found Andrew Painter. When he created Daniel, and I saw him for the first time, it was so exciting. With his illustrations, I started creating the book layout and used the skills I had already been learning in InDesign and Photoshop to design the interior and the cover around his art. I learned the specifics, preparing image files, picking type fonts that suited dyslexia-friendly layouts, and creating separate files for different formats.

Because of the readers of *The Secrets of My Spectrum*, I'm now self-employed as an author and book formatter. Your support and

EDUCATION

recommendations to friends and family have helped me keep writing, and I'm incredibly grateful for that. That is the main reason I decided to write this book. I had requests for years, and at first, I didn't think I had much more to say. I hope this journey with me into the experiences I've faced helps in some way.

I'm not the success story many people would have liked to read about. I didn't take exams. I'm not in a romantic relationship, with a job outside the home, managing to navigate public transport and meeting friends at the weekends, but I'm happy, I'm earning my own money, and I really enjoy signing and shipping my books to readers.

I don't even mind the customer service part, and I'm always on hand to answer emails if someone is concerned about an order. I'll admit I don't get to all my reader emails as quickly as I'd like, but that takes a different kind of brainpower for me.

~ A page for your thoughts ~

FINAL THOUGHTS

I still face challenges in several areas of my life, like public transport. I need support if I have to take a bus or train. Telephone conversations are another huge struggle, and real-time conversations can be difficult because I often debate myself out loud to figure out how I'm feeling or what I think.

Unless I've had time to process my thoughts, I don't always explain myself clearly. Buying clothes on my own is something I still find overwhelming. Decisions feel harder when I'm alone, and I often feel like I'm being watched, which makes it worse. I prefer to go with someone, usually my brother. Even though he's also autistic and struggles in many ways, socially he's more confident, and that helps me. Cooking is another area where I have to be careful. I tend to forget I've put something in the oven and wander off, thinking I'll only be a few minutes, then come back to find I've almost started a fire. I've learned to rely on alarms and remind myself not to leave the kitchen. The same happens in the bathroom. I don't know what compels me to walk away, but I often forget what I'm doing, which can be a real problem.

However, I've also noticed real progress over the years. Getting my driving licence gave me a huge confidence boost and made me much more independent. I didn't realise it at the time, but it was a turning point. For the first time, I felt genuinely free.

Brief social interactions have become easier too. I'm better now with spontaneous conversations than I used to be, as long as I'm not under pressure. Small talk and greetings feel more natural. I still get caught off guard sometimes, but overall, I'm told I handle conversation well, even if I haven't always believed it myself. Food shopping is much easier, especially if I have a list. If I know what I need, I can get in and out of the supermarket without overthinking it. Just don't ask me to pick up anything extra, because if it isn't on the list, I'll forget it.

Looking back, I've realised that many of the things I worried about weren't worth the anxiety. As I step beyond twenty-one and further into adulthood, I'm learning to embrace new challenges, celebrate my progress, and trust in my ability to grow at my own pace. The journey isn't always easy, but every step forward, no matter how small, brings me closer to greater independence and confidence. And if, like me, you're worrying about the future, remember that if the expected routes feel too challenging, you can always make your own.

Books we think you'll like

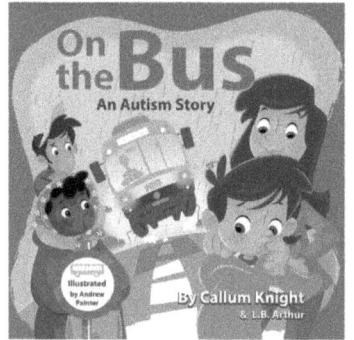 

Framibooks.com

ABOUT THE AUTHOR

Callum Knight is the author of *The Secrets of My Spectrum* and its sequel *More Secrets of My Spectrum, Autism into Adulthood*, heartfelt memoirs that explore his experiences of growing up autistic and navigating the transition into adulthood.

First published at sixteen, Callum's writing has resonated with readers worldwide, offering insight into masking, relationships, education, and self-advocacy. His work is praised for its honesty, clarity, and ability to make complex experiences accessible to families, educators, and autistic individuals alike. Last year, he also created two children's books, which he thoughtfully designed to be accessible for young autistic readers as well as children more broadly. Each title includes interactive elements such as a spot-the-difference puzzle and a colouring page, perfect for those moments when a story alone isn't enough. Every page Callum writes is carefully crafted with autism in mind, ensuring his books are engaging, inclusive, and supportive.

Beyond writing, Callum is passionate about cars, creative learning, and building understanding between autistic and neurotypical communities. He continues to share his journey with authenticity, aiming to help others feel seen, supported, and empowered.

Callum Knight lives with his family in Kent, United Kingdom. Readers can reach him at thesecretsofmyspectrum@gmail.com. For business enquiries, please contact callumknighttsoms@gmail.com.

CRISIS & HELPFUL PEOPLE

Make a note of at least two people who have told you they want you to reach out to them if you need support. These are the people who want to be there for you.

It's okay to ask for help ~ you would want them to contact you if they needed you.

Name _____

Number _____

Name _____

Number _____

If you don't want to talk to someone you know, why not speak to someone you don't?

National Autistic Society
For autistic adults and children, and their families. Website: www.autism.org.uk

Supportline: www.supportline.org.uk

IF YOU HAVE THOUGHTS OF SUICIDE OR SELF-HARM, PLEASE SEEK HELP NOW!

Shout is an affiliate of Crisis Text Line® in the UK that provides free, confidential support, 24/7 via text. It's the first free 24/7 texting service in the UK for anyone in crisis anytime, anywhere. Shout is available in England, Scotland, Wales, and Northern Ireland.
Text SHOUT to 85258 in the UK to text with a trained Crisis Volunteer.

CRISIS & HELPFUL PEOPLE

How It Works - A live, trained Crisis Volunteer receives the text and responds, all from our secure online platform. The Crisis Volunteer will help you move from a hot moment to a cool calm.

Ambitious about Autism
For autistic children and young people, their parents and carers.
Call: 020 8815 5444
E-mail: info@ambitiousaboutautism.org.uk
Website: www.ambitiousaboutautism.org.uk

For my readers in the United States

Text or Call the Lifeline anytime, 24/7 on [**988**] The 988 Suicide & Crisis Lifeline provides free and confidential emotional support to people in suicidal crisis or emotional distress 24 hours a day, 7 days a week, across the United States.

www.ingramcontent.com/pod-product-compliance
Lightning Source LLC
Chambersburg PA
CBHW061219070526
44584CB00029B/3905